D1205014

Akua
is Great

By Dr. Artika Tyner

Text Copyright © 2021 Dr. Artika Tyner

Illustrations copyright © 2021 Planting People Growing Justice Press

Illustrations by Bilal Karaca
Design by Reyhana Ismail

All rights reserved.

No part of this book may be reproduced in any manner without express written consent of the publisher, except in the case of brief excerpts in critical reviews and articles.

All inquiries or sales request should be addressed to:

Planting People Growing Justice Press
P.O. Box 131894
Saint Paul, MN 55113
www.ppgjli.org

Printed and bound in the United States of America
First Edition
LCCN: 2020951643
SC ISBN: 978-1-7351239-0-5

Dedication

This book is dedicated to the scholars of Saint Peter Claver School in the historic Rondo community.

Bedtime is Akua's favorite time.

That's when Akua and Mama read a special book together.

"What makes you **great,** Akua?" asks Mama.

"I am a **Gifted,** proud African Queen!"

"Yes, like Yaa Asantewaa, who gave us the courage and strength to reach our dreams," says Mama.

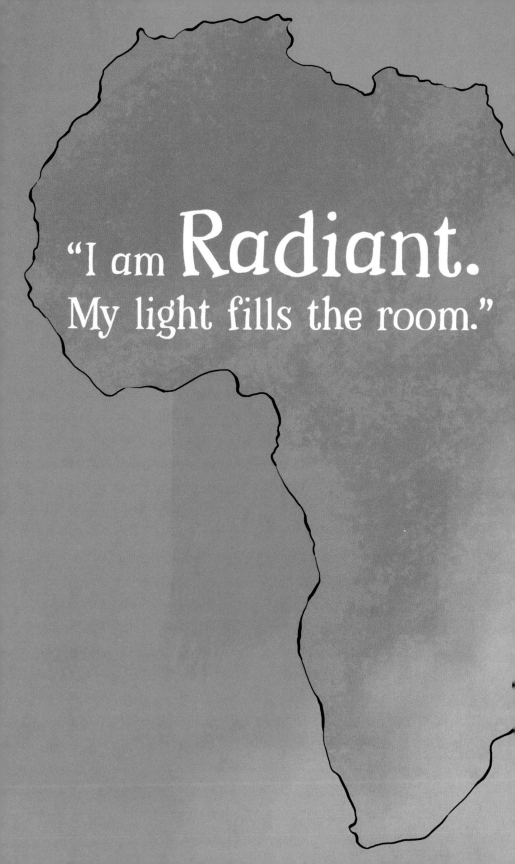

"I am Radiant.
My light fills the room."

"Yes, your beautiful locks and bright smile are magical just like Queen Nanny," Mama says.

"Yes, each day you are exploring, learning, and growing like Francisca Nneka Okeke," says Mama.

"I am Artistic!"

"Yes, you are a talented painter and sculptor like Maria Naita," Mama says.

"I am
Talented!"

"Yes, you can play the djembe, speak Swahili and Twi, and sing, like Miriam Makeba," Mama says.

"Akua, what does it mean to be **GREAT?**" asks Mama.

"I am...

Gifted

Radiant

Eager to Learn

Artistic and

Talented."

Note to Parents and Educators

Daily affirmations can serve as a key tool for promoting self-empowerment and cultural pride. They are a key reminder that our youth are powerful beyond measure.

Help a young child create their daily affirmations:
- Begin by writing 2 "I AM" statements.
- Draw a picture that reflects each statement.
- Post the artwork on the wall as a daily reminder that the child is G.R.E.A.T.
- Learn about leaders who inspire like Yaa Asantewaa or Maria Naita.

Name Chart

The day a child is born is a cherished memory and special occasion. The Akan people of Ghana name their children after the day they are born.

Day	Boy	Girl
Monday	Kwadwo	Adwoa
Tuesday	Kwabena	Abena
Wednesday	Kwaku	Akua
Thursday	Yaw	Yaa
Friday	Kofi	Afua
Saturday	Kwame	Ama
Sunday	Kwasi	Akosua

Short Biographies

Yaa Asantewaa
1840-1921
Ghana

Yaa Asantewaa was a powerful Ashanti queen who fought for the rights of her people against British rule.

Miriam Makeba
1932-2008
South Africa

Mariam Makeba, known as Mama Africa, was a South African singer and civil rights leader.

Maria Naita
1968- 2019
Uganda

Maria Naita was a successful artist who created sculptures and celebrated her rich cultural history through her art.

Queen Nanny
1686-1755
Ghana

Queen Nanny was a military leader who led a community of formerly enslaved Africans called Windward Maroons in the fight for freedom.

Francisca Nneka Okeke
1956-present
Nigeria

Francisca Nneka Okeke is a talented scientist and professor of physics at the University of Nigeria.

About the Author

Artika R. Tyner is also called: "Akua" (born on Wednesday). She is a passionate educator, an award-winning author, a civil rights attorney, a sought-after speaker, and an advocate for justice who is committed to helping children discover their leadership potential and serve as change agents in the global community. She is the founder/CEO of the Planting People Growing Justice LLC.

Dr. Tyner's Daily Affirmation:
I am G.R.E.A.T.
I am Rondo.
I am a writer.
I am an educator.
I am a leader.

PLANTING PEOPLE
GROWING JUSTICE

About Planting People Growing Justice Leadership Institute

Planting People Growing Justice Leadership Institute seeks to plant seeds of social change through education, training, and community outreach.

A portion of proceeds from this book will support the educational programming of Planting People Growing Justice Leadership Institute.

Learn more at www.ppgjli.org

Made in the USA
Monee, IL
28 September 2021

78517725R00017